What's in a Game:

D1279969

What's in a Game:

Play Therapy for Adults

KATHLEEN GRANT, MA, LMFT AND
LAURA OSBORN, PSY.D.

ISBN: 1515125394
ISBN 13: 9781515125396

Kathleen Grant LMFT
608 Independence Avenue SE
Washington, DC 20003
United States

Dedication

To Luke and Tom, the two guys who have been in our corner from the beginning. Here's to you! Thanks so much.

Acknowledgements

WE HAVE TO begin by acknowledging our debt to Luke Hohmann, whose games we have adapted for the field of psychotherapy. Not only did he create the foundation on which we are building, his personal encouragement and direct involvement have resulted in excellent suggestions that have helped us to hang in there and to make this a better book.

We thank our editor, Kathleen Goolsby, for her impressive organization skills with a manuscript that badly needed them. We are grateful to our fellow therapists and friends: Carol Fowler, LMFT, Carlyne Fein, LMFT, and Dana Girard, PsyD,; Edie Culiner, Jeromie Speros, Joseph Pacelli and Sarah Precourt.

Finally, Kathleen would like to thank her husband, Tom Grant, PhD, for his endless patience, encouragement, reading and rereading, contributions to the art work, and willingness to hand hold when needed. Laura also thanks him for everything, except for the last one.

Table of Contents

Foreword

IN 1903 ELIZABETH Magie created a politically inspired board game designed to teach its players that the fair distribution of wealth was superior to the wealth-accumulation tactics employed by the big monopolists of her time — people like Andrew Carnegie and John D. Rockefeller.

Elizabeth's high ideals were not shared by her players, who found far greater enjoyment in using the rules to create monopolies that enabled them to bankrupt their opponents. To add insult to injury, her designs were misappropriated by Charles Darrow, who is wrongly credited as the creator of the game Monopoly®

As a game designer with idealistic goals, I've come to accept that my games have the potential to be misused in ways I cannot imagine. Fortunately, I know of no such adaptations of my games.

Instead, I'm honored by the many ways in which smart, creative, caring, and similarly idealistic people like Kathleen and Laura have adapted my games to solve entirely new kinds of problems.

In this extraordinary book, Kathleen and Laura adapt a number of serious games originally created to solve complex business problems to create breakthroughs in therapeutic care. Weaving game design and game theory with the empathy and wisdom of practice, Kathleen and Laura give you a step-by-step process for leveraging these games in your practice.

And unlike Monopoly®, the games in this book won't cause bankruptcies, damage relationships, or cause tempers to boil over. Instead, the games in this book can help heal families, build relationships and create a foundation for lasting change.

So, get to work, and play some games.

— Luke Hohmann
   Founder and CEO
   Conteneo, Inc.

Introduction

WELCOME TO THE world of serious games! In this chapter, we will introduce you to a new way of helping clients that centers around the use of games. Unlike games designed for entertainment purposes, these serious games are designed to solve specific therapeutic problems through play.

There are precedents in other human endeavors: military institutions use simulation and role play to prepare for battle; in business, simulations stimulate the development of strategic thinking and tactical plans. Serious games continue to help businesses understand their clients better and create products that are more useful; games are also often used in software design to organize the information from the Marketing departments, Customers, and Software Engineers (Hohmann, 2007; Chen & Michael, 2005).

Serious games are even being used in medical research. We are applying those time-tested, practical techniques to psychotherapeutic purposes. Of course, board games and childhood games have been used in therapy for decades, but mostly with children as Play Therapy. (Axline, 1974; Sperling 1997; Landreth, 2012) We believe our book bridges the gap between child and adult therapy with games that combine a serious purpose with a playfulness that softens what can be difficult moments of clinical work.

Here are a few of the possible benefits of using these games in your practice:

- They elicit detailed information for treatment planning.
- They expose unwritten rules clients use in their relationships.
- They defuse emotional reactivity that can swamp a session.
- They uncover the strengths as well as weaknesses in clients' relationships.
- They create a non-blaming structure that lets the parties hear each other and feel heard.

The treatment module we are presenting consists of three serious games:

- **Knowsy®**[1] - a quick way to learn about each individual's priorities, either as a single client or as part of a couple, family, or group.
- ***Speed Boat*** - a visual, effective way to uncover strengths and weaknesses in relationships.
- **Remember the Future** - a means of creating a roadmap for life after therapy.

For readers who would like further details, please contact our website: http://SeriousMindGames.com

Knowsy

---

1 Knowsy® and Innovation Games® are registered trademarks of Conteneo, Inc. Used with permission.

Speed Boat

Remember The Future

There are no winners or losers in these games. Instead, they result in deepening and refining clients' understanding and communications. The games also produce an action plan, which is a natural part of the debriefing after a game ends. In addition, the games can save money, time, and effort by establishing the most efficient way to achieve everyone's goals.

Here are some typical scenarios that we will use throughout the book

• There's the family that wants to help Dad begin the long, difficult road towards sobriety. This family is likely to be shut down and fearful. The substance abuser and the rest of the family are likely to have very different ideas about what to expect from therapy, and quite divergent views about what their new roles and responsibilities will be. **Knowsy®** is a good way to start measuring the degree of alignment and misalignment in this family's expectations; another therapist might want to use ***Speed Boat***, depending on what clinical judgment indicates this particular family would best respond to.

- A couple in distress has their first session with you. Getting a handle on the problems in the relationship can be like walking a minefield - every bit of information elicited from one partner has the potential to spark an explosion of outrage or sorrow from the other. This situation, familiar to anyone who works with couples, is where the serious game **Knowsy®** can aid with the initial stage of treatment planning by defusing some of the emotional reactivity that can swamp a session.

We will be expanding on these examples in the following chapters.

Toolkit

This book is your toolkit for applying the games in your practice. For each of the three games, the following chapters contain:

- A general description of the game and how it works
- Where the game fits into the therapeutic process and how to fit it in treatment planning
- The steps needed to introduce the game to your clients
- Guidelines for how to run the game in a session with your clients
- What to do after a game ends to use it as a stepping stone to the remaining treatment

The games we will be discussing in later chapters share many traits with games with which your clients are already familiar. For example, they have rules, a limited playing time, and a set of actions or moves that each player can take. Then there are the rules that we set out to break, the ones that have helped hold dysfunction in place.

This changing of the rules applies to us, the therapists, as well. We get to move out of the roles that clients may have assigned to us, or that unconsciously we may have taken on ourselves. As we play these games with our clients, we are not the expert, adversary, or arbiter, but rather we are fully present in the moment, letting the game show the way.

1

How Serious Games Enhance
Psychotherapy Treatment

So JUST WHAT are serious games? The most general definition says that a serious game is a game played for purposes other than entertainment. Our purpose has been to create games that allow you, the therapist, to expose and change the implicit rules your clients use in their communications with others, including you. The games are designed to help a couple, family, or group see their issues with each other directly, with a minimum of therapist interpretation. They help save relationships by improving communication between individuals and groups and aid them in coming to a common understanding. And last but not least, they bring an element of fun to a serious purpose.

The serious games we have developed are short activities, with clear beginnings and endings. They complement the longer, more diffuse kinds of interactions more typical in treatment. As therapists engaged in the on-going process of people getting to know themselves and others, we can use these brief games over and over again to coax out more information from partners and families at different times in the therapeutic process.

Benefits to the Therapist

- **Games Discover Client's' Unspoken Relationship Rules with You.** The games will help you change the rules of how you interact with your clients. For example, applying these games in your practice might help you educate clients—in a non-confrontational manner—on why they need to remain in therapy. Or you may discover what you are doing (or not doing) that makes them want to leave. Many of the conflicts in the therapeutic relationship are often not directly addressed; these games offer an easier way to get into those touchy areas.

- **Games Alter the Therapist's Role.** We therapists know that clients can put us in the role of authority or adversary - unhelpful perceptions that build resistance to progress. This is especially true in family therapy, where a couple or family often unites in resistance to change, or in substance abuse treatment where the clients tend to be authority resistant. Serious games powerfully circumvent these problems by creating an entirely new kind of interaction model.

  You get to move out of the parts that clients may have assigned to you or that unconsciously you may have taken on yourself. Thus, the games reduce clients' expectations (and yours!) that the therapist can "fix" one (or any) of the couple, family, or group members.

- **Games Assist in Treatment Planning.** Treatment has a beginning, middle and end, a structure that serious games helps reinforce and integrate. Then there are the realities of insurance for many people that require therapists to plan well to get the maximum benefits for their clients in the number of sessions available. So the more we know, and the sooner we know it, the better.

The following is a brief description of the games and where they can fit into the therapeutic picture:

- **Knowsy®** is good at eliciting detailed information in early sessions, leading to better treatment planning.
- ***Speed Boat*** is especially well-suited to the middle point of therapy, where energy and focus may lag.
- **Remember the Future** uses the lessons gained in sessions to lay out a roadmap for future.

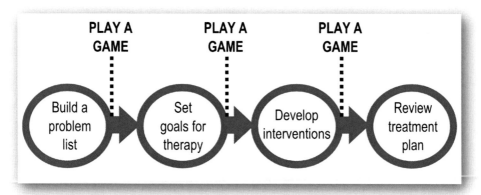

- **Games Engage Participation.** You will elicit detailed information from each client because these games give everyone a chance to play, even the participants who usually stay quiet in other settings or never get a chance to speak. Whether they love to play the games, or resist, whether they participate creatively or narrowly, they will be giving you valuable information about themselves and how they interact with others.

  Sometimes it's hard to know which questions to ask, leaving us not knowing that we don't know about critical aspects of our clients' lives. These may be dark areas for the client as well. Serious games can demonstrate these realities, without the necessity of insight from the client or intuition from the therapist.

Benefits for Clients

- **Games Expose the Unspoken Rules.** Exposing and changing the unspoken rules applies to the relationships of couples, families, and groups. They may have tacit arrangements in place which work like the thermostat in a house. When the temperature is above 76 degrees, the air conditioning comes on; the temperature is below 55, the heat comes on. When a topic arises that creates anxiety, the "thermostat" goes on and drops the topic, which reduces the emotional temperature to a comfortable level. These implicit agreements about what to discuss and what not to discuss act as a thermostat, keeping the house comfortable for the couple, family or group . . . or at least not painfully charged with emotional heat.
- **Games Have Strong Visual Elements.** We humans are highly visual creatures, with strong emotional reactions to the things we see. "A picture is worth a thousand words" expresses a long-standing truth about the way we learn and how we feel. The visual aspects to serious games engages this part of the brain, allowing participants to see and be seen in a way that conversation doesn't always accomplish. The visual artifacts are meant to enhance experience.
- **Games Stimulate the Healing Power of Play.** Never underestimate the value of having fun! Families that play together stay together, or at least come to enjoy each other more and learn how to relax some of the barriers that separate them. Just as these games help identify maladaptive patterns among people, they also demonstrate the strengths and resources people bring to their

relationships. Participants share their priorities, name the strengths they see in themselves and others, plan together for the future. All this fosters trust among the participants.

- **Games Can Speed Up the Pace of Therapy.** Therapy can sometimes feel painfully slow for clients. As therapists, our job includes managing the pace of therapy. Sometimes we wish to move people along faster (rather than letting them wallow in a negative state). Often it takes time for clients to develop insight and lower their resistance to therapy. The games shift the locus of control to them, giving them the tools to break down their own barriers.

Benefits for both Therapists and Clients

- **Games Defuse Emotional Reactivity.** How often have we seen the difficulty a sense of proportion and rational thinking have in penetrating the storm of emotion in our clients' brains (and our own!). Play creates the framework that reduces emotional charges and enables partners or to hear each other and feel heard. In this new paradigm that play has structured, partners or families can explore their hopes, desires, dreams, expectations, and needs.
- **Games Expose the Unknown Unknowns.** Asking the right questions is a valuable therapeutic skill; the capacity to hear and understand the questions is measure of a client's growth. But therapists can dig in the wrong direction, and clients can feel hurt and misunderstood. Games expose the "unknown unknowns," and aid both client and therapist in recognizing what they don't know about their relationships.
- **The Games are Flexible.** It's easy to adapt the serious games presented in this book to a variety of settings. As you get used to using these tools, you'll customize them for your particular couples,

families, or group challenges. Switch them around, modify the rules, use them in different orders - they are yours to play with.

The same flexibility benefits the clients, who should be encouraged to use these games outside the therapeutic setting. They can and should learn to play them without a therapist, without any special equipment, as the needs of the moment dictate.

- **Games Create Tangible Products.** These games create physical artifacts to which the partners or family members can refer in later discussions. For both therapist and client(s), they create a concrete visualization of issues that may have felt abstract or disconnected. These products are a natural basis for an action plan, which can incorporate both written documents and graphics.

(Optional) A recording of the game session, which can be another useful reference for future discussions. Recordings often capture important interactions that the partners or family members might otherwise miss, or not be able to fully digest in the moment.

2

Overview of the Games

THE TREATMENT MODULE we present consists of the three serious games we have already introduced. We suggest the following order in which to use the games to best reinforce the therapeutic phases. However, the games' inherent flexibility allows you to use them at other appropriate therapeutic moments.

- **Knowsy®** is a game that is especially good at eliciting the detailed kind of information that is so useful to have at the beginning of therapy, as we plan approaches and interventions. Although **Knowsy®** is indicated for intake and early sessions, it can be usefully employed at almost any point in therapy that the clinician chooses, especially when sorting out priorities becomes an issue.
- ***Speed Boat*** is a game especially well-suited to the middle point of therapy, where energy and focus may lag. It creates a balanced picture that takes into account both strengths and weaknesses in a relationship. Grounded in the realities of the present, it opens the way to honest assessment and course correction.

- **Remember the Future** uses the lessons gained in therapy to lay out a roadmap for future. Often emotional reactivity becomes an issue as clients approach the end of therapy. **Remember the Future** is designed to contain and channel these emotions, both as therapy ends and the post-therapeutic reality begins.

The games' rules are behaviorally and cognitively oriented. For example, the lists that participants create in the games of **Knowsy®** or *Speed Boat* are not tallies of any participant's character flaws. The very act of stating priorities and naming what moves relationships forward and what holds them back implies attainable changes individuals can achieve through concrete action.

The mood is positive, solution focused, and present focused. The structure of the games implies that things can get better, facilitating the installation of hope that is critical to the early phase of treatment.

Fitting the Game to the Situation

It's easy to fit the serious games presented in this book to a variety of settings. As you get used to using these tools, you'll customize them for your particular couples', families', or group's challenges.

For example, we have already indicated that the suggested order in which the games are used is actually quite flexible. Although **Knowsy®** is indicated for intake and early sessions, it can be usefully employed at almost any point in therapy that the clinician chooses.

Although their inherent flexibility means they can be used at other appropriate therapeutic moments, these games are often used when the therapist is looking for a creative solution, or if the therapy process seems to plateau or becomes contentious.

Remember those scenarios we first mentioned in the Introduction? Here they are again, where we can use them to illustrate how to use the games with different client configurations and at different points in the therapeutic process:

Scenario 1: Alcoholic Dad and his Co-Dependent Family

This is the client family with alcohol and recovery issues. Both the identified patient (Dad) and the rest of the family are likely to have very different ideas about what to expect from therapy, and quite divergent views about what their new roles and responsibilities will be.

Knowsy® can be used to assess the family during intake; it can be used later in therapy to judge the degree of alignment about the meaning and outcome of treatment between the alcoholic and the family; it can be used as therapy is ending as a way to illustrate to the family the progress they have made in understanding each other.

Speed Boat can help with a family that thinks they can drop the alcoholic off in rehab, pick him/her up later "cured" and either start or resume a happy family life. *Speed Boat* makes graphically clear the dense web of interconnection among all members of the family, and areas of weakness that will not be fixed by changing one person. *Speed Boat* can work well in the middle of therapy, especially when the chemically-dependent individual has been sober for a while, and the family members feel their "support" is less important. This game will illustrate the true needs of the family unit, and the illusory nature of support in this context.

Remember the Future can be quite helpful for this family towards the end of therapy and treatment. Many families in this situation believe now that their loved one is no longer drinking, the problems they suffered before will just disappear. This game is a powerful way to illustrate that old issues don't just disappear, and additionally, they are entering a new reality that will continue to demand things of them.

Scenario 2: The Couple in Distress

During their first session with you, you find out they are struggling with infidelity, money issues and basic lack of trust. Coming to therapy is a last-ditch effort; neither individual holds out very much hope for the marriage. However, they have built a successful business together, which they would like to see continue.

Knowsy®: A therapist might use this game to judge what is most important for this couple - do they really want to save their marriage, or do they think they must preserve their marriage in order to maintain their business. **Knowsy®** could be an excellent way for them to understand each other's priorities, and for the therapist to put the energy and effort into the couple's real goals.

Speed Boat is another way to clarify this important issue. The couple may see that not only do they have many more anchors than propellers in their marriage, but that the anchors are qualitatively more important that the propellers. This can lead to the realization that what they really want is a way to end their marriage amicably, or as amicably as possible.

Remember the Future can help this couple create a clear picture of how they want their future relationship with each other to look, especially as it is likely that other romantic or marriage partners will emerge at some point. Staying on good terms requires much more than just good intentions. This game can help prepare the couple for that reality, and plan the legal and social steps necessary for the outcome they want.

We will see these clients again, as we will expand on these scenarios in Chapter Four ("About **Knowsy®**"), Chapter Five ("**About Speed Boat**"), and Chapter Six ("About **Remember the Future**"). We will take you through a detailed explanation of how to set up, run, and conclude the games, using our hypothetical clients' problems to illustrate what we mean.

3

How to Run the Games

THIS CHAPTER DEALS with the information and rules common to all three games. Rules that are specific to one game alone are covered in that game's chapter.

Before starting a game with a couple, family, or group, the therapist ideally will have had a chance to review the general guidelines and the specific suggestions for running each game. However, in clinical work we don't always have the option to do this. Emotions may run too high, or the moment might be lost if time is spent reviewing the rules. As always, clinical judgment and appropriateness are your best guides. All that said, we suggest the following steps when starting a game, especially if it is for the first time:

- Review the guidelines in this chapter.
- Explaining to your clients why you are using a serious game as a tool to help them may or may not be useful, depending on the needs of the client. You may want to move your clients into the game quickly, without getting into discussions about why you are

doing this. If they play the game and feel its benefit immediately, the "why" is self-evident.

- Do carefully explain how to play the game. Keep it simple; the games are not complex, and should be presented as enjoyable and useful exercises

Guidelines for the Therapist

Here are some guidelines for successfully using serious games in a clinical setting.

1. Prepare, prepare, prepare. That includes both rehearsing the game yourself as well as ensuring you have all the materials needed.
2. If you decide to video the game session, you will probably need another person to help you.
3. Always, always save the lists, drawings, Post-it® notes, and any other physical products of the game. They are helpful later in a debriefing session or for review of progress.
4. Enforce time limits. Many of these games work because the restrictions of time compel people to behave in unfamiliar ways. For example, if a couples is used to hours-long arguments, a 15-minute time limit for a game may actually force them to say more, or say it more clearly, than they would while getting lost in hours of words.
5. Ensure that each participant creates a separate list or Post-it® notes. No conferring at this point. Keep clients from playing the role of gatekeeper, no matter how helpful they're trying to be; otherwise, the quiet and cautious players won't say everything they need to.

6. Don't push the game if it's not working. A "failed" game can still be a success. The game is just a tool to produce new clinical material. If you decide to end the game early, but the participants learned something from the experience, then the game isn't really a "failure." Even if a participant walks out of the game, you, the clinician, will learn a good deal about how that person interacts when under stress.

7. You need to be very clear about what issue/problem the serious game addresses. For example, "The family" is a very big and very vague construct. Something more specific, such as, "How the family deals with major life changes, like a new job," is more likely to achieve useful results.

8. You may want to write the issue/problem somewhere on the board. Sometimes you need to ask the players to state the issue/problem as a goal. For example, "How the family deals with major life changes" is a less effective way of saying, "All members of the family need to make adjustments to major life changes, even if they're not the ones experiencing the change directly." For one member it may be a change of location; another may focus on the shifting financial situation.

9. Be ready to improvise, perhaps with some slight adjustments to the rules governing the games. Subsequent chapters will give you more concrete ideas on how to improvise in the context of the games.

General Rules for the Game Participants

Below are the general rules that you will need to explain up front and enforce with your clients who play a game. Use the general rules that apply to any psychotherapy group, such as explaining the guidelines that govern the goings-on in the group clearly before beginning. The points below are more particular to the games.

1. Save the expression of your feelings about what you have heard at the end, not during the list-making or Post-it® note creating phase.
2. You may ask questions that clarify what was said.
3. You may ask for more information or the meaning behind what was said.
4. Accept that there will be strict time limits. (Of course, if someone constantly violates time limits, or just has a hard time holding to them, an important avenue of clinical inquiry has opened to you. Always remember, the game is only the means to information not otherwise as easily obtained.)

Dealing with Objections

Most people enjoy these games, as they remove confrontation and blaming and they are interesting to play. However, this is not always the case. Prepare for occasional resistance ("This game is stupid." "Why are we doing this?" "This is a waste of time."). Here are some suggestions on how to handle these situations.

Remember that the goal of the game is not the game but, rather, the uncovering of clinical material. Instead of forcing the situation, explore it. Anger usually masks other, more vulnerable emotions. Is your client sad? Afraid? Hurt? How do the other family members handle this person's negativity, sarcasm, and criticism? You can learn a lot about the family hierarchy, its unspoken roles, and rules at a moment like this. Some members of the couple, family, or group may refuse to participate. Here are some suggestions if that happens.

- Encourage players to see more than the negative.
- If one of the partners in a couple refuses to participate, you might not want to run the game since you normally need more than one person to play.
- If you are working with a family or a group, the refusal of any one member to play the game requires delicate handling. If possible, try to get consensus on how to proceed. For example, is everyone pretty much okay with the non-participating member sitting apart from the others and remaining silent but contributing to the discussion in the end? Remember, the game itself is not your goal; the aim is to uncover patterns, systems of control, the nature of the family or couple hierarchy, and how the family or couple maintains homeostasis.
- The refusal to play the game may be an attempt to sabotage a possible change to the status quo or possibly a fear-motivated

response to a feeling of being exposed. Of course, the refusal to play has already exposed something; just don't assume that you know what it is. A compassionate and non-defensive therapist has a great opportunity to explore with everyone present (including the refuser) how this kind of pattern may have played out in the past. Who resents this behavior? Who might be secretly relieved?

- Some participants may walk out. Depending on your clinical judgment, you may ask that person to return or let him/her cool off for a while. Or you can shelf the game for the time being and focus on the reactions of the remaining participants. Are they afraid of the anger that may have been displayed? Are they anxious about the sadness or abandonment they see implied in the act of leaving? What have you just learned about the unspoken rules of this couple or family?

- Sometimes, even when the game elicits powerful emotions, you may wish to keep the participants playing. If you are concerned that some players may be too shy or cautious about what they say, seat the players some distance from each other before the game starts.

What to Do After the Game Ends

Some clinicians write a report, some do debriefing sessions, some do both. The order does not matter. These are only suggestions; it is up to your clinical judgment.

Keep the materials produced during the game. Don't throw away the drawings, Post-its®, and other materials that players create during the game. These are important artifacts of the game that you and your clients will refer to later.

Guidelines for Follow-Up Sessions.

There is no set rule to how many follow-up sessions are necessary. It may take a couple of sessions to completely review a game, depending on the number of participants and the richness of the information obtained in the game. Use your clinical judgement and use as many or as few follow-up sessions as you wish.

How You Know You're Succeeding

You will know the games are successful when you begin to see some of the benefits mentioned in Chapter One coming to fruition. The participants become more engaged and they begin to trust that the therapeutic process can actually work.

There are other important ways that these games will affect your sense of success. You may see dynamics that weren't apparent to you before or aspects of your clients about which you were unaware. This, in turn, has a direct effect on how you plan treatment and how you understand the relationship to the couple, family, or group you are treating.

4

❓ About Knowsy®

KNOWSY® (PRONOUNCED *NOZEE*) is a wonderfully easy way to open a meaningful dialog among a couple, family, or group, especially in the early stages of therapy. The **Knowsy®** game is a tool that gathers information that might not otherwise become available for a long time.

The Alcoholic Dad and his Codependent Family Play Knowsy®

As an example of the benefits of using **Knowsy®**, let's expand on Scenario 2 (first mentioned in Chapter 2) to see how you can use this game to identify the degree of alignment on priorities within a client group:

That family of a long-time alcoholic has finally persuaded Dad to enter treatment, and they want to help in the long, difficult road towards sobriety. They are together in your office for intake, listening to you explain what they can expect in the days and weeks ahead.

Instead of starting with a list of do's and don'ts, you hand each family member a sheet of paper and say, "We are going to play a short game about priorities." You ask them to list in order of importance their five biggest fears about entering treatment. (Alternatively, you could have a pre-made list of five priority items and ask each family member to rank them in order of importance.)

Next you ask them to create "guess-lists"—one list per family member, ranking in order of importance what they think are each family member's five biggest fears about treatment (or, for the alternative method, list the five priority items of each member).

You then ask the family members to compare their lists. This can yield surprising (to the family) results. For example, the alcoholic may list financial strain or time apart as the biggest concern. Other families may rank the possible loss of the alcoholic to the disease or to suicide as their biggest fear.

The elicitation of the mental models of others through the "guess-lists" drives therapy, as you will identify the misperceptions that can cause strain. The power of **Knowsy®** is that it uncovers how well the individuals in a group understand each other's priorities and identifies the degree of alignment on priorities within a group. How much do they agree on what is important? Do different family members have different hopes for the outcomes of treatment? The game may illuminate issues no one realized. Sometimes a family member might list a high-priority item that surprises the other family members, and sometimes they surprise themselves.

For example, a priorities list about fears that family members have concerning the recovery process might include the loss of importance. Codependent spouses often discover, sometimes to their shock, that their role in an alcoholic family provides them with admiration from others and the feeling of being essential that is hard for them to give up.

Playing **Knowsy®** uncovers in just a few minutes critical data points that would take hours using traditional techniques. You can then sketch out the initial phase of treatment, operating from much more accurate information about each individual and the family as a whole.

How the Game Works during the Session

Playing **Knowsy®** instills hope in your clients, with the resultant trust that is important early on. It does this because it allows your clients to express themselves and hear each other in a way they may not have before. Because this happens early in the therapy process, the experience becomes a rewarding one more quickly than normal.

You also can use **Knowsy®** just for fun. Each time your clients play **Knowsy®**, they will focus on a topic you select, or one they choose. If, for a change of pace, you use a topic like Favorite Ice Cream Flavor or Favorite Pizza Topping, you can inject much-needed levity into complex, stressful situations.

Why Only Five Items to Prioritize?

There is an important reason for limiting the priorities list to only five items. Extensive testing by Conteneo®, the creator of **Knowsy®**, has shown that three items are too few, seven items are too many, and even numbers don't create a strong sense of priority. Five items makes prioritizing difficult enough but not too difficult, and the resulting discussion can be rich for a couple, family, or group.

Guidelines for Choosing the Game
Topic and Items to Prioritize

There are several methods for creating the lists of priorities:

1. You determine the topic and the associated list of items to prioritize. Use this method when you're concerned that the players, especially the patient, will avoid critical topics. For example, you might select "Favorite Kind of Vacation" as the topic for a couple engaged in couple's therapy. Your list of associated items for your clients to prioritize might include relaxing on a beach, sightseeing in a major city, visiting lots of museums, anything without kids, camping with the family, road trip, etc. Or the items associated with a topic of a happier married life might include better communication, dealing with children or in-laws, resolving money issues, desire for greater intimacy, and equitable division of household duties.

2. You determine the topic and the patient determines the list of associated items to prioritize. You can use this method when your patient feels the others are not listening to his/her needs.

3. You determine the topic and each participant makes his/her list of priority items.

4. You determine the topic and all the players jointly contribute to creating the list of items to prioritize. In this method, you as the therapist might want to spark the brainstorming by suggesting some topics, with the understanding that the participants can cross out any item and replace it with one of their own. You need to facilitate this process and make sure they keep the list to no more than 15 items, which they ultimately must narrow down to five items they all agree on.

Remember, as we have mentioned elsewhere in this chapter, you can have the clients choose the topic. It can be quite informative to see what they would like to explore. You can also decide which client (VIP = Very Important Person) chooses the topic, depending on your clinical aims. Do you need to reinforce parental authority? Do you want to encourage a silent client who is always getting talked over? Let them choose the topic and then discuss his/her list first.

Materials You Will Need

1. Whiteboard, butcher paper tacked to the wall, or flip chart
2. Paper or a large Post-its® pad and a pen for each participant
3. (Optional) Video camera (or mobile phone with video capabilities), operated by a person in the role of a second facilitator (you as the therapist are the primary game facilitator). A drawback to this approach is that individuals often act quite differently when they know they are being recorded, which can result in less spontaneity and authenticity. Recording can be a good idea when a client remains oblivious to negative patterns of behavior after they have been repeatedly pointed out.

How to Play Knowsy®

1. After a topic is chosen, a list is generated, either by the therapist, VIP, other clients, or some combination thereof. The VIP orders the items on the list, starting with the most important and ending with the least important, and gives it to the therapist.
2. The therapist writes the list on the board in no particular order, keeping secret the order in which the VIP has listed each item.
3. The rest of the spouse, family, or group attempts to guess the order in which the VIP has put the items.

Exploring Game Results:

Next, you and your clients explore the results of the game, with you as the moderator of the discussion. All players post their lists on a whiteboard or butcher paper on the wall and each player discusses the reasons behind the priorities/order they chose. This discussion helps improve the understanding of their priorities and whether they are aligned so that you can help them build a shared priority.

As guidelines, here are some questions for the results-exploration discussion:

1. Did you struggle to prioritize your list of outcomes of what you want from therapy? If so, what made it difficult?
2. Was it difficult or easy to make the first list? What helped or impeded?
3. What kinds of emotions did you experience when I asked you to make the list?
4. What triggered those emotions?

5. Did you experience any physical feelings?
6. What images came to mind?
7. What was it like for you to hear what the other players think is important?
8. What does communication mean to each of you?
9. What does [a particular item on the list] mean to that person?
10. Is communication merely a matter of accurately conveying information?
11. Does communication mean getting what you want when you ask for it?
12. Is communication about being heard in some deeper way?
13. Was something important missing from the list?

If your clients are a couple who each created their own lists (as VIPs), now is when it makes sense to have them compare their lists to gauge how close together or far apart they are on important matters.

What to do After the Session

You now have a wealth of information from the game to use in shaping future therapy sessions, or as a way to shape the bigger picture of treatment planning. If you recorded the game, you may review the video with each participant individually, with all the participants together, or both.

How to Adapt Knowsy® for Your Purposes

Knowsy® is a highly flexible tool that can work well at any point in the therapeutic process, and is highly effective at helping you find out what you don't know, and therefore would not have asked about. Some examples:

- You can use Knowsy® in the middle of therapy to compare clients' responses with the ones at the beginning of therapy as a way to show them how much they have changed, grown, or come to an understanding. This will build therapeutic trust (that is, the couple, family, or group trusts in your ability to help their situation).
- Knowsy® is a wonderful way to help the parents and siblings of a disabled child. Often the siblings' needs are neglected in favor of the disabled child, and the parents are overwhelmed. This is a way the siblings can be truly heard.
- For the truly brave, it can be a way to get a deep look into the therapeutic relationship itself, played between you as the therapist and your clients. How do your clients really see you? Friend? Expert? Killjoy? The voice of reason? The possibilities are endless; but fortunately the **Knowsy®** list is limited to five items.

The more you use the **Knowsy®** game, the more its flexibility and adaptability to a variety of clinical needs will become apparent. Feel free to experiment!

Suggested Timeline

This timeline is based on a typical 50 minute session.

Time Needed	Task Performed
10 minutes	Check - in with each family member (when an Orientation has been done prior to a family session).
5 minutes	Explain the rules of the game and hand out materials.
5 minutes	They make their own lists
5 minutes	Family members guess each other's priorities.
25 minutes	Explore the game results
That is the end of the 50 minute session.	
10 minutes	The therapist takes notes and decides what to do with the information unearthed in the **Knowsy®** session.

5

About Speed Boat

SPEED **B**OAT IS a serious game well suited to the middle phase of treatment. By now you have a fairly clear sense of the dysfunctional picture, and significant therapeutic time can pass without much seeming to happen. During this plateau phase it can be helpful to play **Speed Boat**.

Alcoholic Dad and his Co-Dependent Family Play *Speed Boat*

A typical situation in the dreaded plateau phase might sound something like the following.

> Therapist: "It sounds as though things are going better now. Ryan's problems at school seem to have subsided and it isn't so tense at home. You have talked about maybe taking some time off from therapy."

> Mom: "Yeah, maybe we need some time off. We've been coming for about six months now, and our problems seem under control at the moment - Stan isn't drinking and has been good about going to meetings. It just doesn't feel like we have anything new to report."

Dad: "Ryan has football practice and I am going to be traveling for business."

Therapist: "There is something I would like us to try today. We're going to play a short game called **Speed Boat**, which is about identifying what's working for you and against you as a family. **Speed Boat** will help us get a fuller picture of how each of you see yourself and the family as a whole."

The therapist in this scenario uses **Speed Boat** to gently direct the family towards the idea that there is a lot to do that is not necessarily on the surface.

The therapist draws a picture of a boat on the whiteboard with a waterline. She passes out Post-its® and pens to the family and asked them to write the positives (propellers) and negatives (anchors) in their family life.

As the family finishes each Post-its® they put them up on the board above the waterline for the propellers and below the waterline for the anchors. When everyone is done, the family has created a picture of their present situation that clarifies what they need to do next.

When your clients believe everything is fine or fine enough, your attempt to help clients recognize such hidden patterns can sometimes put you in the role of adversary or make it seem that you are trying to prevent them from leaving therapy.

If they still decide to end or suspend therapy, ***Speed Boat*** is a valuable tool for helping them plan their life post therapy.

How the Game Works during the Session

The sense of direction and energy ***Speed Boat*** can provide applies equally to clients' therapeutic goals, the therapeutic process, and the therapeutic relationship itself. What is hindering forward momentum? What would give the clinical hour more energy and movement forward?

It is a chance for the client to identify to you, the therapist, what may be lacking in your relationship. This is a conversation few clients are willing to have with their therapists, but ***Speed Boat*** provides a safe, non-blaming way for each individual to ask for what he/she needs. In this case, one would use the ***Speed Boat*** exercise with the questions: "What is slowing down my therapy?" and "What is helping my therapy?"

While many people have complaints about their relationships, most really want to make them work well. However, it's a normal human tendency to make complaint after complaint after one gets started talking about the relationship. Additionally, many of us simply do not know how to ask for what we want from someone without phrasing it as a complaint or criticism.

Speed Boat helps to counterbalance the tendency to blame by asking for positive feedback rather than just complaints and by stating dissatisfaction in impersonal terms rather than as the fault of the other(s). This helps the participants remember just what drew them to that relationship and what keeps them in it.

Materials You Will Need

1. A picture of a boat. The picture needs to be at least 2 feet wide by 2 feet high. You want something large enough so that the players can put Post-its® on the picture without having to overlap them.

2. A large piece of butcher paper pinned to a wall or a large flip chart on an easel to hold the *Speed Boat* picture and Post-its®. (Alternatively, you could draw a picture of a speed boat and water on a whiteboard.)

3. A Post-it® notes pad for each participant. Use the standard size (2 inches by 2 inches), which is big enough for the players to write several words without having to resort to very tiny lettering.

4. Pens for each participant. Dark-colored felt-tipped pens are better because it's easier to see the writing from a distance.

5. Camera (to take a picture of the speed boat with the Post-its® in place).

How to Play *Speed Boat*

The game uses a large picture of a speed boat on water. Place the picture on a large piece of butcher paper pinned to the wall, or on a large flip chart on an easel, or draw one on a white board.

You (or, alternatively, you and your clients) first choose a topic for the game. Try not to be overly broad. For example, "Things you think are hurting and/or helping your relationship in this family/group" is not as focused as "What is helping maintain sobriety in our household right now, and what is making it more difficult." Distribute a pad of Post-it® notes to each player.

Tell your clients there is a time limit of 5 minutes for this game and you'll give them a warning at the halfway point. Remind them that the reason for the time limit is to allow focus on quality, rather than on quantity, of their responses.

At the end of the time, The Post-its® will be placed on the picture of the speed boat, as follows:

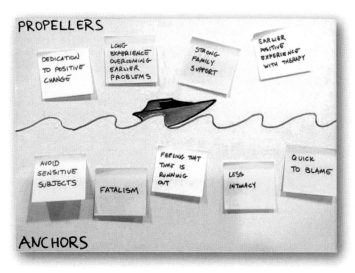

1. The factors that participants believe speeds their relationship forward are "propellers" and positioned above the water line. Put the most helpful items (Post-its®) directly on the boat. These are the strengths and opportunities that increase the likelihood of relationship success.

2. The factors that participants believe hold the relationship back are "anchors" and positioned below the waterline. The greater the hurt described, the lower the Post-its® anchor is positioned on the picture. These are the things that weigh the relationship down and hinder it from succeeding.

Variations: You can use different sizes of Post-it® notes (small, medium, and large) for the propellers and anchors to indicate the size of the problem or impact of a propeller's help. Or you can segment them by timelines or by priorities (such as short term and long term). Also, some clients who play this game sketch out a destination for the boat.

Exploring Game Results

Next read each Post-its® and decide with the couple, family, or group how to place them in categories/headings. Most often, these categories will suggest themselves, as recurring variations on themes will appear on the Post-its®. Seeing a heavy concentration of Post-its® grouped together is a powerful clarification of your client(s)' situation. Your knowledge of your clients will help this process. As an example, some categories/headings that naturally arise include communication, money, children, in-laws, intimacy.

Here are some suggested guidelines for this discussion.

1. Are there mismatched expectations?
2. Did a goal mean one thing to one person and something else to another?
3. Do the participants misunderstand the definitions of "success" or "failure?"
4. Notice if/where there are clusters of positives and negatives.
5. Are there surprises? Are there hidden reefs that bog down the relationship or unexpected tides that move things along?

Don't forget about the process of the game. The process is always as important, if not more so, than the content. What was it like for the participants to do this exercise? Was it difficult because someone's mind went blank or because it produced anxiety or sadness? Was it gratifying for a participant to realize his/her strengths that had been previously ignored? Was it energizing to see more clearly where they need to apply efforts?

This activity pushes the participants to look at the positives they might otherwise ignore or minimize. It can be a way to gauge real progress, as they may realize they now have "accelerators" they didn't possess a few months, or even a few weeks, ago.

Finally, the process of exploring and discussing the game results implicitly recognizes the importance of planning. Not all anchors can be cast off at once; not all accelerators can operate at the same time. By learning to prioritize and making the changes that allow casting off and accelerating to continue, participants deepen the skills they gain in therapy.

Before ending the game session, take a picture of the *Speed Boat* board with all of the Post-its® in place.

What to do After the Session

You now have a wealth of information from the *Speed Boat* game to use in developing an action plan for addressing your clients' problems. *Speed Boat* invites the practical work of problem-solving.

Here is when you invite your clients to prioritize and open the way to solutions. The sense of proportion you help to establish during this process helps your clients understand that they can't address the problems all at once. This, in turn, gives them the chance to have successes they can build on, rather than feeling stuck with an overwhelming mess of interconnected issues.

Basically, the action plan encompasses ways to dissolve the anchors and strengthen the propellers. Here are some suggested ways for you and the couple, group, or family to review each propeller and anchor to develop an action plan.

- Prioritize the anchors and propellers. When deciding what to work on first, (or even just what importance to give the issues that have been identified) this is where the idea of using small, medium, and large Post-its® comes in handy. Alternatively, you can ask the participants to vote on the prioritization of each anchor or propeller.

- You can distribute a weighted-score spreadsheet to the participants. Some therapists use a simple 1, 2, 3, 4 as in a Likert rating scale; and some use a weighted score.
- The weighted scores can open the discussion to how much physical and emotional pain, money loss, frustration and waste an anchor causes the participants. The positive scores help create the optimism and self-confidence needed to carry out successfully an action plan.
- Sometimes players think they've exhausted their lists of anchors and propellers before they really have. You may need to do some coaching if you suspect that's the case.

How to Fit the Information from the Game into Treatment Planning

As mentioned earlier, **Speed Boat** is uniquely well suited to the middle phase of therapy, where clients (and the therapist!) can lose focus. This midway position allows for taking stock of improvement that might not be obvious, and at the same time points towards the future by showing what remains to be done. All this can deepen confidence that the therapeutic process has been working and will continue its usefulness through what can be the middle-phase doldrums.

Clients often enter therapy in great distress, and when that pain starts to lessen somewhat, you as the therapist need to educate them about how to use the clinical setting to get at underlying patterns of communication and behavior they need to address. Often, they even need to understand that those patterns exist.

Speed Boat graphically depicts the interlocking complex of positive and negative elements that constitute your clients' emotional and communications systems.

How to Adapt *Speed Boat* for Your Purposes

You can use this game in group therapy settings, couple's sessions, family sessions, or multi-family/group sessions. It is best to have more than one person in the session, with an upper limit of twenty people. However, *Speed Boat* has been used successfully with groups as large as thirty people.

This game can stand on its own or along with other serious games. Although we have suggested its use in the middle phase of therapy, it can be played at any phase of the therapeutic process. For example, for clients who may be more visually oriented, it can take the place of Knowsy® during intake and early assessment. Finally, *Speed Boat* works with just about any topic the therapist or client might want to address in session. How is planning for retirement going? What's working better in your relationship with your children? After achieving a certain amount of clarity on the priorities, what is in the way of their realization? What has helped them come to pass?

This is an easy, practical game to play that presents participants with a balanced picture of their relationship. It helps all participants (and the therapist) see things more completely, including the positive aspects – which are all too easy to ignore or take for granted as they don't need "fixing."

Suggested Timeline

This timeline is based on a typical 50 minute session.

Time Needed	Task Performed
5 minutes	Check - in with each family member
5 minutes	Explain the rules of the game and hand out materials.
5 minutes	The couple, family, or group writes down their propellers.
5 minutes	The couple, family, or group writes down their anchors.
5 minutes	They put the Post-its® up on the board (or the therapist does)
5 minutes	The therapist leads a discussion to categorize the Post-its®
20 minutes	Explore the game results
That is the end of the 50 minute session.	
10 minutes	The therapist takes notes and decides what to do with the information unearthed in the *Speed Boat* session.

6

Remember the Future

THIS SERIOUS GAME is well suited to the last stage of therapy when you and your clients have reached therapeutic goals and the therapy relationship is coming to an end. It can help shape the last weeks and set the positive, therapeutically grounded basis for client independence. This works equally well for clients who are leaving too soon, or who must stop due to money, insurance, family problems, etc. Creating a plan for the future may help clients see they aren't ready to leave, or give clients who must stop an ongoing connection with therapist until therapy can be resumed full-time. Some therapists may choose to stay in touch through monthly check-ins.

This game does not require *imagining* the future, but *remembering* it – a distinction that is crucial to making this technique work. The couple, family, or group has goals, established at the beginning of therapy and clarified over time with the help of serious games such as Knowsy® and **Speed Boat**. The focus of this final serious game is not on the goal but, rather on the means of getting there. This focus answers such questions as "What concrete steps would these clients have needed to take to reach the outcome they desire?" and "What kind of help will they have needed from other people?"

Alcoholic Dad and his Co-Dependent Family Play Remember the Future

Dad has been in treatment now for a year, and the other family members have paid attention to their own needs and behaviors through attendance at therapy and support groups. Although everyone is feeling pretty hopeful, there is an undercurrent of mixed euphoria and fear. They have begun to remember what good family life can be like. The old, bad balance has been broken, and the new arrangements are still fragile.

> Mom: "I'm so proud of all he has accomplished. And I know I am not supposed to try to manage his recovery, but I get so scared if I think he is going to miss an AA meeting."

> Kid: "Gee Mom, why don't you give him a break? Everything is going to be just fine. Can't you see how hard he is trying?"

> Dad: "I know I am supposed to focus on my own recovery, but I can't help but feel the weight of my wife's fears and my son's hopes."

This is the kind of situation **Remember the Future** is made for. It gives this family the means to imagine what kind of family they want for themselves and what kind of person each individual wants to be – not in the present time but in the future. However, this act of the imagination runs backwards from that future point where goals have been realized and reverses through all the steps, efforts, and changes required to get where they want to be – which started back in what is now the present.

So the therapist explains the difference between setting goals and re-membering, and asks the family to name the most important thing they want to remember.

Dad: In the future I am remembering, I have been able to focus on my own needs for sobriety, and not the needs of my family. For this to hap-pen, my family will have taken care of themselves by their commitment to regular attendance at Al-Anon and Al-Ateen. I will have formed impor-tant friendships and relationships in sobriety, especially with my sponsor.

Mom: In the future I am remembering, I have been able to trust my husband again. I don't feel the need to check up on him, or constantly scan for the signs that he has been drinking. This is in large part be-cause we have practiced rigorous honesty with each other, in things large and small. Honesty has become a policy and a habit.

Son: In the future I am remembering, I was able to become a kid again, instead of worrying about my parents all the time. This was because my parents learned to turn to each other for help and support, and not to me.

This gives you an idea of how the game might start. Now each participant needs to flesh out those decisions and activities that helped lead to the changes they are "remembering."

How the Game Works During the Session

Remember the Future is easier than trying to plan the future, because in this game the goals have already been accomplished and clients are only reminiscing about how and when they were achieved. It lessens stress by allowing clients to create plausible sequences of events that accomplish the goal, even if these events have not yet occurred.

This is an opportunity to employ rich visualization and attention to detail. It is not the moment for broad brush strokes or general statements of intent. The couple, for example, that intends to take more time for each other, in part because that helps them communicate better, may realize they need to get reliable child care to allow them to spend time alone on a date. To achieve this goal, in the game they might "remember" that they adjusted their family budget by replacing expensive coffee purchased at a coffee shop with coffee made at home. They might also "remember" that they agreed to replace expensive birthday presents with a simple cards of affection.

The structure of the game enables them to remember that, even though they were giving up previously enjoyed items, they did not feel resentment because they enjoyed their time together *more* than these items.

Much like building a city whose blueprint needs to be drawn first in detail, clients must lay the foundation for the life they want. There is an infrastructure to build, a sense of how to allocate resources, and some fall-back plans for when life inevitably throws a curve.

The implicit message embedded in this serious game is that the clients are capable of taking responsibility for themselves and their relationships and that they have the tools to do so. All too often, therapy merely ends with some recapitulation and statements of intent. **Remember the Future** helps move all parties through the final stages of therapy with a positive,

optimistic, practical and realistic basis for independence that remains therapeutically grounded.

Materials You Will Need

1. Butcher paper (pinned to the wall), a whiteboard, or a large flip
   chart on an easel, which you will use for drawing the timeline
   (and optional swim lanes). How far into the future the participants wish to go dictates how much space you need to draw
   the timeline. It needs to be long enough to encompass the present point to the future date. Leave space above and below the
   timeline to place participants' Post-it® notes. There needs to be
   enough space to enter all of the activities necessary to meet the
   participants' goals.

2. Post-its® pads for each participant. Use the standard size (2 inches
   by 2 inches), which is big enough for the players to write several
   words without having to resort to very tiny lettering. You may use
   a different color of paper for each participant or use the same color
   for everyone.

3. Pens for each participant. Dark-colored felt-tipped pens allow you
   and the participants to better see the writing at a distance.

   a. (Remember to use the same colors and size of paper and
      same ink color if the participants want to be anonymous.)

4. Camera (to take a picture of the finished timeline with Post-its®).

How to Play Remember the Future

This is a three-part game, and there is a fifteen-minute time limit for each part.

Part 1. In the first part of this game, the participants define their goal(s) by writing them on Post-it® notes, and they put the notes on the timeline. It is important to be very clear and specific, ensuring that everyone knows what the goal(s) means to them.

Generally, the couple, family, or group chooses a point of time in the future and a description of what their life together looks like as if they are remembering it. Some go forward six months, some push it out to a year; beyond that there tend to be too many variables. The future date is really up to the participants but also needs your practical guidance as the therapist.

After determining the future date, participants need to agree upon what their life will look like at that point in time. Here are some sample questions they can ask themselves to get a picture of that future point.

1. What have we been doing for work, hobbies, our financial life and retirement, school, social life, religion/spiritual life, and our immediate and extended family?
2. How did our life change for the better or worse?
3. To whom did we get closer?
4. From whom did we distance ourselves?
5. What material possessions did we obtain and what did we do with them?
6. What material possessions did we let go of?

Part 2. In the second part of this game, participants imagine they are truly at that future point and remembering how they got there. They write on Post-it® notes the steps they "remember" that they took to achieve the goal(s). What they "remember" are actually the tasks they will need to do to achieve their goals. Here are some questions they may ask themselves to determine the tasks/steps.

1. What sacrifices will I have made for my family (that will not have caused resentment within me)?
2. What will I have made time for (given work, health, energy, age, etc.)?
3. How will the goals and dreams I have – along with everyone else's goals and dreams – fit into the family structure?
4. How will the goals and dreams I have – along with everyone else's goals and dreams – benefit others?
5. How will the goals and dreams I have – along with everyone else's goals and dreams – ask for sacrifices from others?
6. How will I have successfully supported others in the family structure as well as myself?

It is helpful to ask participants to picture themselves at the age when the goal has been reached. They need to keep in mind that *all* the actors in the system will age.

Each participant may write as many Post-it® notes with the "remembered" steps as he/she wishes within the fifteen-minute time limit for this section of the game.

The goals can be different sizes (small, medium, large), depending on their priority. Also, it is possible to have parallel goals, such as working on establishing financial goals and emotional intimacy at the same time.

Part 3. You and/or the participants then position their Post-it® notes along the timeline according to category and priority within that category and in the appropriate order to achieve that goal. Some therapists allow the participants to put their own Post-it® notes on the timeline.

As an alternative to just using a timeline to the future date, you may find it helpful to draw multiple timelines or swim-lanes to capture the groups or organizations your client(s) will "remember" leveraging in the pursuit of the goal(s). For example, consider an addict in treatment who is also under medical care for Type II Diabetes. You might encourage this client to add a swim-lane for his/her doctor(s), adding Post-it® notes on how those doctors will have helped your client(s) achieve their goal(s).

Exploring Game Results

Playing **Remember the Future** results in developing an action plan for achieving the participants' goals. Once the participants agree on all the goals and tasks to achieve the goals, you need to record this information in an action plan.

It may take a few sessions for the action plan to gel, and it's possible that other therapeutic issues may arise during this process.

The action plan needs to specify who is responsible/accountable for tasks and when. In the process of developing the action plan, your clients may disagree over how and when certain tasks should be performed, who should do them, etc. This is a great opportunity to explore and polish communications skills, recognize unintended messages one participant is sending to another, etc.

To develop the action plan, ask the following questions.

1. By what dates do milestones or tasks need to happen to achieve goal on time? It is a good idea to establish a schedule with regular updates, progress reports, etc., for all participants.
2. Who will perform each task?
3. What are the individual milestones to achieve to reach the goals?
4. What are the necessary resources and sacrifices?
5. What are the specific action tasks for each milestone, goal and achievement?
6. How will the individuals perform specific action tasks given limited time, money, and energy?
7. What tools are necessary (planning tools, flowcharts, etc.)?

The action plan also needs to specify how the participants will reward themselves for their achievements. Just what will those rewards be once they reach the milestones, achievements, and goals? Think about creating small, medium, and large rewards for small, medium, and large achievements.

It is important to celebrate success when meeting milestones instead of just checking off a goal and moving to the next item. This helps keep everyone motivated and reinforces success. Clients who have been struggling through hard times may need to relearn (or learn) the value of fun and positive self-acknowledgement.

What to do After the Session

Now to the question and answer time! What was it like to play this game? Was there anything that surprised you, either from yourself or another person? Do these goals seem realistic? Does this vision of the future seem enjoyable? Are the actions necessary to get there achievable? Remind your clients that both the personal and the group goal must be acknowledged and included in the action plan.

If there are videos you may find it beneficial to review them from the **Remember the Future** session or earlier serious game sessions such as *Speed Boat* to further revise the action plan.

How to Fit the Information from the Game into Treatment Planning

Playing **Remember the Future** is an opportunity for all participants to discuss their intentions for the future of the couple, family, or group and create a strategy that will bring it about. This exercise will help formulate methods to help the couple, family, or group reach the goals they identified during the course of therapy. After all, there was a reason the couple, family, or group was formed in the first place.

At the end-stage of therapy, it is important to develop a plan that helps ensure success of the work done in the sessions. Even when therapy has ended, you can schedule regular reviews of **Remember the Future** and the resulting action plan as a way to maintain a working relationship with a couple, family, or group. This will lessen the damage if a crisis emerges, and you also can address and resolve the crisis more quickly. In the middle of a crisis, it is rather difficult to break in a new therapist, establish trust, and deal with the problem.

How to Adapt Remember the Future for Your Purposes

Remember the Future can be used at the beginning of therapy (especially useful for Brief Therapy practitioners) if the insurance company sets an end-date to the client's therapeutic time. The clients may also set an end-date and can use this game to decide what they wish to accomplish in the sessions. In fact, **Remember the Future** can be used at any point in therapy when a client feels stuck or a certain goal seems hard to attain. For clients who need help with planning and organization, this game is especially useful.

Also, this can be used internally with staff to set goals and timelines for the agency.

Suggested Timeline

This timeline is based on a typical 50 minute session.

Time Needed	Task Performed
5 minutes	Explain the rules of the game and hand out materials.
5 minutes	The couple, family, or group decides on the end-date & goals.
10 minutes	The couple, family, or group write up their Post-its®.
15 minutes	The couple, family, or group discusses the priorities and how to achieve the goals.
15 minutes	Explore therapeutically their reactions to the game results
That is the end of the session.	
10 minutes	The therapist takes notes and decides what to do with the information unearthed in the **Remember the Future** session.

7

Final Words of Advice

ABOVE ALL, KEEP in mind that the game is not the thing! Don't get caught up in thinking that a game and its rules are what is really important, and that if your clients don't follow the rules, the game isn't working.

The games discussed in this book are meant to evoke emotional information from your clients. In other words, it's really all about the process. Using these games will help you get to the information that you don't know, as well as what you don't know you don't know.

Please rely on your clinical judgment at all times; if you need to vary the rules of the game, go ahead! Finally, enjoy these games - they can of course be played for therapeutic purposes, and they can be played for fun. They can alter the conversation, help create breakthroughs, make new narratives, and last but not least, teach the healing power of play.

The final great advantage the games give you are genuinely measurable outcomes. Knowsy, for example, generates measures of alignment that you can compare, upon entering treatment, and right before leaving it. We will be publishing further details about the ways to use these games for measuring outcomes on our web site, http://www.seriousmindgames.com.

Cheat Sheet:

How to Play Knowsy®

1. After a topic is chosen, a list is generated, either by the therapist, VIP, other clients, or some combination thereof. The VIP orders the items on the list, starting with the most important and ending with the least important, and gives it to the therapist.
2. The therapist writes the list on the board in no particular order, keeping secret the order in which the VIP has listed each item.
3. The rest of the spouse, family, or group attempts to guess the order in which the VIP has put the items.

How to Play *Speed Boat*

1. Choose a topic, or help your clients choose one.
2. The factors that participants believe speeds their relationship (or any other issue the therapist and clients want to explore) forward are "propellers" and positioned above the water line. These are the strengths and opportunities that increase the likelihood of success.
3. The factors that participants believe are holding back success in a given area are "anchors" and positioned below the waterline. These are the things that weigh the issue down and hinder it from succeeding.

How to Play Remember the Future

1. The participants define the future they want in rich detail.
2. In the second part of this game, participants imagine they are truly at that future point and remembering how they got there. They write on Post-it® notes the steps they "remember" that they took to achieve the goal(s). What they "remember" are actually the tasks they will need to do to achieve their goals.
3. Each participant may write as many Post-it® notes with the "remembered" steps as he/she wishes within the fifteen-minute time limit for this section of the game.
4. You and/or the participants then position their Post-it® notes along the timeline according to category and priority within that category and in the appropriate order to achieve that goal. Some therapists allow the participants to put their own Post-it® notes on the timeline.

Bibliography

Books

Aldrich, C. (2005), *Learning by Doing: A Comprehensive Guide to Simulations, Computer Games, and Pedagogy in e-Learning and Other Educational Experiences.* San Francisco, CA: John Wiley & Sons Inc.

Axline, Virginia (1974), *Play Therapy.* New York: Ballantine Books.

Brown, S. (2009), *Play: How It Shapes The Brain, Opens The Imagination, And Invigorates The Soul.* New York, NY: Avery.

Hohmann, Luke (2006), *Innovation Games: Creating Breakthrough Products Through Collaborative Play.* Boston: Addison-Wesley.

Huizinga, John (1955), *Homo Ludens: A Study Of The Play Element In Culture.* London: Routledge & Kegan Paul, Ltd.

Landreth,Garry (2012), *Play Therapy: The Art of the Relationship.* London: Routledge & Kegan Paul, Ltd.

Michael, David and Chen, Sande (2005), *Serious Games: Games That Educate, Train, and Inform.* Boston: Cengage Learning.

Charles Schaefer (2002), *Play Therapy With Adults*. Hoboken, NJ: John Wiley & Sons.

Journal Articles

Li, M., and Tsai, C. (2013), "Game-Based Learning in Science Education: A Review of Relevant Research." *Journal Of Science Education And Technology*, Vol. 22, Issue 6.

Girard, C.; Ecalle, J., and Magnan, A. (June 2012), "Serious Games as New Educational Tools: How Effective Are They? A Meta-Analysis of Recent Studies." *Journal of Computer Assisted Learning,* Vol 29, Issue 3.

Spinka, M., Newberry, R., and Bekoff, M. (2001), "Mammalian play: training for the unexpected." *Quarterly Review of Biology*, Vol 76, Issue 2.

Journals

Games For Health Journal (http://www.liebertpub.com/overview/games-for-health-journal/588/)

International Journal Of Game-Based Learning (http://www.igi-global.com/journal/international-journal-game-based-learning/41019)

Organizations

Every Voice Engaged (http://everyvoiceengaged.org/)

Games For Health (http://www.liebertpub.com/overview/games-for-health-journal/588/)

Serious Games Association (http://www.seriousgamesassociation.com/)

Serious Games Initiative (http://www.seriousgames.net/)

Web sites

Serious Mind Games (http://seriousmindgames.com)

Serious Games At Work (http://seriousgamesatwork.org)

About the Authors

KATHLEEN GRANT IS a licensed marriage and family therapist (LMFT) who has worked in mental health organizations and private practice. Kathleen's work has focused on trauma, addiction, and family systems. She holds a Masters in Counseling Psychology from the University of Notre Dame de Namur, a Ph.D. in political science from the University of California at Irvine, and Level 2 certification in EMDR. She currently lives in Washington, DC, in a 150 year old house on Capitol Hill, with a husband, a cat, and a dog.

Laura Osborne also has worked in mental health organizations. She holds a Psy.D. and a Masters of Arts in Clinical Psychology from the Wright Institute, and is a certified hypnotherapist. Her Masters thesis was a case study of a combat-wounded veteran, and her dissertation studied controlled clinical trials of the efficacy of motivational interviewing in a dual-diagnosis population. Laura currently lives in the San Francisco Bay Area with two dogs, three chickens, and her son, and she practices urban farming and sustainability.

Kathleen and Laura have written another book, soon to be published, that is designed to help therapy patients get the most out of their 50 minute sessions.

Made in the USA
Coppell, TX
03 December 2020